THE OPEN UNIVERSITY

Mathematics: A Third Level Course

Numerical Computation   Unit 4

Practical Unit I

The Open University Press

Course Team

Chairman:	W. Y. Arms
Central Members:	P. A. Blachford
	T. M. Bromilow
	F. C. Holroyd
	P. G. Thomas
Staff Tutors:	M. Kennedy
	J. E. Phythian
B.B.C.:	J. A. Richmond
	R. I. Clamp
Student Computing Service:	F. L. Irvine
	M. B. Haywood
Consultants:	L. Fox (University of Oxford)
	H. P. Williams (University of Sussex)

The Open University Press, Walton Hall, Milton Keynes.

First published 1975.

Produced in Great Britain by
Technical Filmsetters Europe Limited, 76 Great Bridgewater Street, Manchester M1 5JY.

ISBN 0 335 05653 9

This text forms part of the correspondence element of an Open University Third Level Course. The complete list of units in the course is given at the end of this text.

For general availability of supporting material referred to in this text, please write to the Director of Marketing, The Open University, P.O. Box 81, Milton Keynes, MK7 6AT.

Further information on Open University courses may be obtained from The Admissions Office, The Open University, P.O. Box 48, Milton Keynes, MK7 6AB.

1.1

Contents

		Page
4.1	**Introduction**	4
4.2	**Computer Packages**	5
4.3	**Packages for Units 1 to 4**	8
4.3.1	Non-linear Equations–$NCROOT	8
4.3.2	Systems of Linear Equations–$NCSLE	10
4.4	**A Worked Example**	15
4.5	**Problems**	19

Appendix—Valid BASIC **Expressions for Input to Packages** — 22

Summary Sheets–$NCROOT — inside back cover

$NCSLE — inside back cover

4.1 INTRODUCTION

This is the first of four practical units in the course. It consists of a number of problems on the material of *Unit 2, Non-linear Equations*, and *Unit 3, Linear Equations*. Your task is to examine each problem and to find out as much as possible about it. The following are the sort of questions you should be asking, but you should not expect to be able to answer them all for each problem.

(i)   Is this problem well-conditioned or ill-conditioned?
(ii) Which method, if any, is suitable for this problem?
(iii) If several methods are suitable, which is preferable?
(iv) Can you think of any modifications to the methods or reformulations of the problem that improve the solution?
(v)   What is there about this problem that gives it its distinctive characteristics? Can you think of other problems with similar characteristics?

You will often find that your solution breaks down into four main steps: **explore** the problem, **plan** your attack on it, **calculate** answers, **analyse** the results. Exploring the problem may involve sketching a graph or tabulating a function, scaling data or rearranging the rows of a matrix. Planning your attack is the work you do before going to a computer terminal such as deciding on the methods and starting values to use. Analysing the results will involve checking that the solution satisfies the original problem and seeing how sensitive it is to changes of data. In section 4.4 there is a typical example of these four stages which is drawn from Television Programme 1.

To help your investigations several weapons are available. Some of the problems are similar to standard problems which can be found in many text books. Some useful books are given as recommended reading at the beginning of Units 2 and 3. You can experiment on these problems, using your calculator or the Student Computing Service. Section 4.3 specifies two computer packages that we have written for you. It should not be necessary to write your own programs.

Your tutor has been specially briefed to help with your practical work. He has a set of hints for each of the problems in section 4.5. Make use of him by writing to him or telephoning to discuss the approach that you have made to the problem and receive his suggestions. Several of these problems may be set as part of your tutor marked assignment. See the *Assignment Booklet* for details. For these problems your tutor is authorized to give you simple hints without deducting marks from your final solution.

4.2 COMPUTER PACKAGES

Library programs for this course consist of packages to tackle specific mathematical tasks. The detailed specifications of individual packages are given in the practical units, but check the supplementary material for notification of any modifications. The instructions for running library programs on the Student Computing Service are given in the *Student Computing Service Users Guide*. If you are not familiar with the material in the guide you should obtain a copy and read it now.

Most of the packages provided for this course have the following outline.

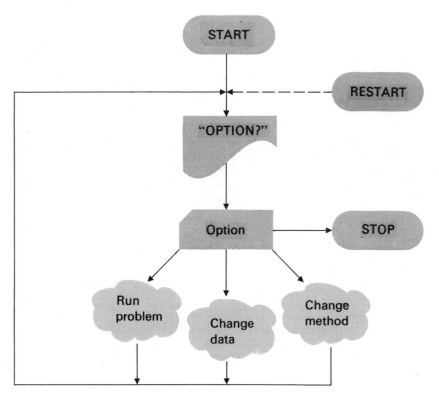

The program revolves around the **option point**. At the option point you have the choice of running the problem, changing the data or method of solution, or stopping. Two important points to note are as follows.

(i)   If the program types

OPTION ?

and you type

Ø

the program will **list the options** that are open to you.

(ii) If you ever stop execution of the program by using the **BREAK** key or **CTRL** and **C** (as described in section 12 of the *Student Computing Service Users Guide*) you can **restart** by typing

RUN-1ØØ

This takes you directly to the option point as shown on the flow chart. Any data that you have already typed in will be saved by this procedure.

Options

Each option is identified by an **option number**. To select an option, type the corresponding option number. The program prints a brief message to identify the option. If further input is required it will then prompt you by typing a question mark. After each option (except stop) the program returns to the option point.

5

On return to the option point all data and parameters that you have input are saved and available to be used again. For example, if you wish to solve the same problem but with a different method you can change the method by using the corresponding option and rerun the problem.

Some of the option parameters are set automatically by the program to a predetermined value. This is known as the **default value**. For example the iteration limit on the package described in section 4.3.1 has a default value of 20. An option is available if you wish to change the value from the default value.

For each package we have provided a tear out sheet at the end of the unit which lists all the options. In general there are the following five categories of option.

Control Options

Control options are numbered between 0 and 9. Options 0, 7, 8 and 9 have special significance.

```
0 —  print a list of available options

7 —⎫
    ⎬ list the data, method and/or parameters
8 —⎭

9 —  stop
```

Options 1 to 6 depend on the package being used.

Problem Options

Options numbered between 10 and 19 are used to submit problems or to change problems.

Method Options

Options numbered between 20 and 29 are used to choose the method used to solve the problem.

Parameter Options

Options numbered between 30 and 39 are used to submit parameters, such as stopping criteria, initial values and so on.

Print Options

Options numbered between 40 and 49 specify the quantity of output.

Functions

Some problems require functions to be input. In reply to the query

```
F(X) = ?
```

you should type the function as you wish it to be computed. Your input must be a valid BASIC expression using the variable X (see the appendix). For example, to input the function

$$f(x) = \sin x - \left(\frac{x+1}{x-1}\right)$$

type

```
SIN(X)-(X+1)/(X-1)
```

To input

$$f(x) = x^3 - 5x + 3$$

type

```
X↑3 - 5*X + 3
```

or, for more efficient evaluation with fewer rounding errors, type

```
(X*X-5)*X+3
```

Sometimes you may wish to look at a family of functions. For example, in section 4.5, Problem 5 is to look at how the largest root of $\sin x - ax = 0$ changes with a. In this case when the program types

```
F(X) = ?
```

you reply

```
SIN(X) - A*X
```

An option is provided to set A to a selected value before attempting to evaluate the function. If this facility is used the parameter must be called A. No other symbols are permitted.

4.3 PACKAGES FOR UNITS 1 TO 4

4.3.1. Non-linear Equations—$NCROOT

The library program $NCROOT is a package to find roots of $f(x) = 0$ by the methods of *Unit 2, Non-linear Equations*. Parts of this package were used in Television Programme 1, but the input and output were modified to fit neatly onto a television screen. An example of how to use this package is given in section 4.4.

The package is based on the outline flow chart on page 5. It revolves around an option point and after every calculation or other operation, control returns to the option point. The following options are provided. They are summarized on a tear out sheet at the end of this unit.

Control Options

0 Print the List of Available Options

This prints a list of the options and returns to the option point.

1 Run the Problem

This runs the problem using the data and parameters previously input. If some required parameter or data has not been provided the program prints a message and returns to the option point.

8 List the Problem

This lists the problem, data and parameters previously input.

9 Stop

This stops the program.

Problem Options

10 Input Function

If you select option 10, the program types

        F(X) = ?

You can respond by typing a BASIC expression using the variable X and optional parameter A (see appendix). The maximum length of expression is 72 characters. The problem is to look for roots of $f(x) = 0$.

Some problems have already been provided for you. For one of these standard problems, after the message

        F(X) = ?

you type the name of the problem.

11 Input Derivative

For the Newton–Raphson method you must specify the derivative. After option 11 the program types

        F'(X) = ?

and you type the derivative.

12 Set Function Parameter A

If the functions specified by options 10 or 11 involve the optional parameter A, it must be set to a numeric value using this option.

Method Options

20 Tabulate

Tabulates the specified function between x_0 and x_1 (set by options 30 and 31) at intervals specified by option 32.

21 Bisection Method

Finds the root of $f(x) = 0$ by the bisection method beginning at x_0 and x_1 (set by options 30 and 31). The stopping criterion is specified by option 35 and the stopping tolerance, ε, by option 33. The values of $f(x_0)$ and $f(x_1)$ must have opposite signs.

22 Newton–Raphson Method

Finds the root of $f(x) = 0$ by the Newton–Raphson method, with first estimate x_0 (set by option 30). The stopping criterion is specified by option 35 and the tolerance, ε, by option 33.

23 Secant Method

Finds the root of $f(x) = 0$ by the secant method, with first two estimates x_0 and x_1 (set by options 30 and 31). The stopping criterion is specified by option 35 and the tolerance, ε, by option 33.

24 Adaptive Method

Finds the root of $f(x) = 0$ by a combination of the secant and bisection methods which is described below. The routine uses the first two estimates x_0 and x_1 (set by options 30 and 31). The stopping criterion is specified by option 35 and the tolerance, ε, by option 33. The values of $f(x_0)$ and $f(x_1)$ must have opposite signs.

25 General Rootfinder

This routine combines the tabulation and adaptive routines. Within an interval specified by x_0 and x_1 (set by options 30 and 31) it evaluates the function f at intervals specified by option 32. If f changes sign between two tabular points the adaptive routine is used to find a root if one exists. This is repeated for each sign change found in the interval.

Parameter Options

30 x_0

This parameter specifies the initial estimate x_0. It is always required.

31 x_1

This parameter specifies x_1. It is required for all methods except the Newton–Raphson method.

32 Number of Intervals

The tabulation routine divides the interval $[x_0, x_1]$ into the number of equal sub-intervals specified by this parameter. The function f is tabulated at the end points of each subinterval. This parameter is required for the tabulation and the general rootfinder.

33 Stopping Tolerance

This specifies the tolerance, ε, used in the stopping criteria.

34 Iteration Limit

This parameter specifies the maximum number of iterations. If this number is exceeded the program returns to the option point. If not specified, a limit of 20 iterations is assumed by *default*.

35 Stopping Criterion

There is a choice of three criteria:

1—Residual. Stop if $|f(x_n)| < \varepsilon$
2—Step size. Stop if $|x_n - x_{n+1}| < \varepsilon$
3—Both residual and step size. Stop if $|f(x_n)| < \varepsilon$ and $|x_n - x_{n+1}| < \varepsilon$

The tolerance, ε, is set by option 33. If no stopping criterion is specified explicitly the program assumes criterion 1, the residual, as the *default* value.

Print Options

40 Full Print

If this option is chosen the program prints a summary of each iteration and the final solution. This option is selected by *default* unless specified otherwise.

41 Print Solution Only

If this option is chosen the program prints only the solution.

Restart Procedure

After pressing either the BREAK key or CTRL and C the program can be restarted, without loss of data, by typing

    RUN-100

Outline of the Adaptive Method

The adaptive method begins with an interval in which the function, f, changes sign. Thereafter it always records an *interval*, I, which is the smallest interval so far discovered in which f changes sign. The *current best estimate* is the end point of I at which f is smallest in absolute value. Each iteration is either a bisection using this interval or a secant iteration using the last two values calculated, which will not necessarily involve a change of sign. Since the secant method is, in general, more powerful than bisection it is always tried first. The iterations are monitored and the routine switches to the method of bisection if one of the following occurs:

(i)   a secant iterate is calculated outside the interval I;

(ii) a secant iterate is calculated which differs from the current best estimate by more than half the width of the interval I, in which case the midpoint of I is likely to be a better estimate.

4.3.2   Systems of Linear Equations–$NCSLE

The library program $NCSLE is a package to solve the system of equations $\mathbf{Ax} = \mathbf{b}$ by the methods described in *Unit 3, Linear Equations*. The maximum number of equations is 15. The package is based on the outline flow chart on page 5. It revolves around an option point and after every calculation or other operation, control returns to the option point. The following options are provided. They are summarized on a tear out sheet at the end of this unit.

Control Options

0 Print the List of Available Options

This prints a list of the options and returns to the option point.

1 Solve the Problem Ax = b

This solves the problem $\mathbf{Ax} = \mathbf{b}$ using the data and parameters previously input. If some required parameter or data has not been provided, the program prints a message and returns to the option point. The method of solution is specified by options 20 to 25.

2 Iterative Refinement

This option carries out a single iterative refinement on the solution using double precision arithmetic. The problem must have already been solved by method 20, 21 or 22.

3 Invert A

This option uses Gauss Elimination on the matrix

$$[\mathbf{A} \mathbf{I}]$$

followed by back substitution to evaluate the inverse of **A**. The method of solution is specified by option 20, 21 or 22.

4 Decompose A

This option decomposes **A** into the form

$$\mathbf{A} = \mathbf{LU}$$

where **L** is lower triangular and **U** is upper triangular. The method of solution is specified by option 20, 21 or 22.

7 List the Data

This lists the matrix **A** and vector **b**.

8 List the Method and Parameters

This lists the method and parameters.

9 Stop

This stops the program.

Problem Options

The matrix **A** and vector **b** can be entered in several ways.

(i)   If the problem is dense, that is most elements of **A** and **b** are non-zero, input **A** using option 11 and **b** using option 12.

(ii) If the problem is sparse, that is most elements of **A** and **b** are zero, use option 13 to input the non-zero elements of **A** and option 14 to input the non-zero elements of **b**.

(iii) To save you time typing in data, we have set up a file of problems for you. These problems are selected by option 15.

10 Specify Number of Equations

This option sets n, the number of equations, which must be between 2 and 15.

11 Enter A

This option is used to input the entire matrix **A** one row at a time. When prompted by the message

        ROW 1 ?

type in all elements of row 1 separated by commas. Too few or too many elements will produce an error message and an instruction to retype the **entire** row.

12 Enter b

This option is used to input the entire vector **b**. When prompted by the message

        ELEMENTS ?

type the elements of **b** separated by commas. Too few or too many elements will produce an error message and an instruction to retype the **entire** vector.

13 Edit A

This option is used to change individual elements of **A**. If **A** has not been set previously, the routine begins by setting the entire matrix to zero. If any elements of **A** have been submitted previously they are left unaltered, except for those changed by editing. The option edits one element at a time, by asking you to specify the row, column and value. For example the following sequence sets a_{52} to have the value -23 and a_{31} to the value 6.

```
EDIT ?5,2,-23
EDIT ?3,1,6
```

To return to the option point, when the program asks

```
EDIT ?
```

type

```
Ø
```

14 Edit b

This option is used to change individual elements of **b**. If **b** has not been set previously, the routine begins by setting **b** to zero. If any elements of **b** have been set previously, they are left unaltered except for those changed by editing. This option edits one element at a time, by asking you to specify the row and value. To return to the option point, when the program asks

```
EDIT ?
```

type

```
Ø
```

15 Standard Problem

This option selects a prespecified **A** and **b** which are already stored on the computer system. To choose a problem, type its name when requested by the program. Subsequent editing of the problem is possible using options 13 and 14. The names of the available problems are given in section 4.5.

Method Options

20 Gauss Elimination with Partial Pivoting

This option selects Gauss elimination followed by back substitution. Each pivot is chosen as the largest element of the current pivot column.

21 Gauss Elimination with User Pivoting

This option selects Gauss elimination followed by back substitution. The program stops after each stage of the elimination and asks the user to provide the next pivot.

22 Gauss Elimination with Essential Row Interchanges Only

This option selects Gauss elimination followed by back substitution. Successive pivots are the elements on the main diagonal of **A**, except that if the corresponding element is zero an essential row interchange is made with the next non-zero element.

23 Jacobi Method

This option selects the Jacobi method, using the first iterate specified by option 30 or option 31 and the stopping tolerance, ε, set by option 33.

24 Gauss–Seidel Method

This option selects the Gauss–Seidel method, using the first iterate specified by option 30 or option 31 and the stopping tolerance, ε, set by option 33.

25 Successive Over Relaxation

This option selects the Gauss–Seidel method with successive over relaxation as described in *Unit 3*, section 3.7.3. The first iterate is specified by option 30 or option 31 and the stopping tolerance, ε, is set by option 33. The relaxation factor, ω, is set by option 32.

Parameter Options

30 Enter x_0

This option is used with iterative methods to input the first trial solution vector x_0. When prompted by the message

     ELEMENTS ?

type the elements of x_0 separated by commas. Too few or too many elements will produce an error message and an instruction to retype the **entire** vector.

31 Edit x_0

This option is used with iterative methods to edit the first trial solution vector, x_0. If x_0 has not been set previously, the routine begins by setting x_0 to zero. If any elements of x_0 have been set previously, they are left unaltered except for those changed by editing. This option edits one element at a time by asking you to specify the row and value. To return to the option point, when the program asks

     EDIT ?

type

     Ø

32 Relaxation Factor

This parameter specifies the relaxation factor, ω, used in the Successive Over Relaxation method.

33 Stopping Tolerance

This is used to input the stopping tolerance, ε, for iterative methods. The iteration terminates if for some $x^{(r)}$, each element satisfies

$$|x_i^{(r)} - x_i^{(r-1)}| < \varepsilon$$

34 Iteration Limit

This parameter specifies the maximum number of iterations allowed in solving a problem by an iterative method. The *default* value is **20**.

35 Number of Iterations Between Print

For iterative methods, the outline print set by option 41 prints out a summary of every kth iteration, where k is set by this option. The *default* is **10** iterations between printout.

Print Options

40 Full Printout

This option gives a full printout after each main step.

41 Outline Printout

This option gives an outline printout after each main step. It is the *default* option. For the iterative methods it prints out the current solution after every kth iteration where k is set by parameter **35**.

42 Print Solution

With this option, only the solution is printed.

Restart Procedure

After pressing either the BREAK key or CTRL and C the program can be restarted, without loss of data, by typing

    RUN-100

4.4 A WORKED EXAMPLE

In Television Programme 1 and *Unit 2* we look at the problem

$$x^3 - 5x + 3 = 0$$

Faced with the problem of finding the largest root of this equation you might proceed as follows.

Explore the Problem

The equation is a cubic curve. It therefore has either 1 or 3 roots. Tabulating a few points near the origin gives the following.

x	$f(x)$
-3	-9
-2	5
-1	7
0	3
1	-1
2	1
3	15

Since there are three distinct changes of sign the cubic equation has three roots and the largest is in the interval $(1, 2)$.

Plan the Attack

So long as a suitable starting value can be found the Newton–Raphson method will be suitable.

$$f(x) = x^3 - 5x + 3$$

$$f'(x) = 3x^2 - 5$$

The iteration function is

$$g(x) = x - \frac{f(x)}{f'(x)}$$

$$= x - \frac{x^3 - 5x + 3}{3x^2 - 5}$$

On the next page there is a sketch of this function g and the function x. For convergence we want

$$|g'(x_0)| < 1$$

and x_0 must be greater than the discontinuity of g at $x = \sqrt{5/3} \simeq 1.29$

$$g'(x) = 1 - \frac{(3x^2 - 5)^2 - 6x(x^3 - 5x + 3)}{(3x^2 - 5)^2}$$

$$= \frac{6x(x^3 - 5x + 3)}{(3x^2 - 5)^2}$$

At $x = 2$, $g'(x) = 0.24$. Hence $x_0 = 2$ seems a sensible starting value.

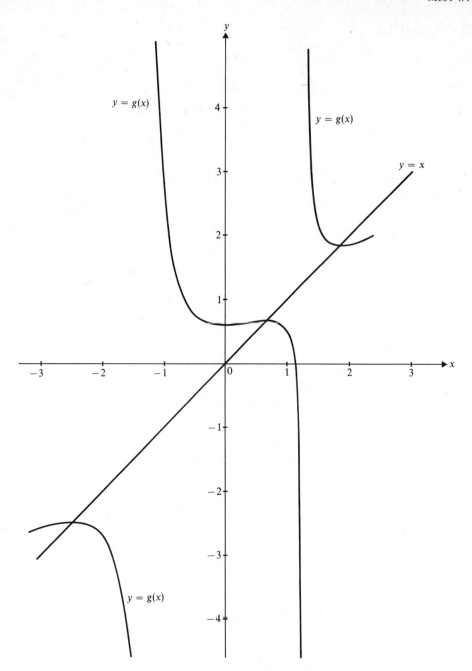

Calculate Answers

Here is the package $NCROOT used to find this root. In this example the data typed by you at the terminal is printed on a grey background.

```
GET-$NCROOT
RUN
$NCROOT


OPTION ?20
TABULATE


OPTION ?10
F(X) = ?(X*X-5)*X+3


OPTION ?30
X0 = ?-3
```

Function in nested form

```
OPTION ?31
X1 = ?3


OPTION ?32
NUMBER OF INTERVALS = ?12


OPTION ?1

TABULATE

  X                   F(X)
 -3                  -9
 -2.5                - .125
 -2                   5
 -1.5                 7.125
 -1                   7
 - .5                 5.375
  0                   3
  .5                  .625
  1                  -1
  1.5                -1.125
  2                   1
  2.5                 6.125
  3                  15


OPTION ?22
NEWTON-RAPHSON METHOD


OPTION ?1

NEWTON-RAPHSON METHOD
F'(X) = NOT SPECIFIED
STOPPING TOLERANCE NOT SPECIFIED
```

More
data required

```
OPTION ?11
F'(X) = ?3*X*X-5


OPTION ?33
TOLERANCE = ?.0001


OPTION ?2.5
INVALID OPTION


OPTION ?30
X0 = ?2.5
```

Set starting
value

OPTION ?1

NEWTON-RAPHSON METHOD

N	X	F(X)
0	2.5	6.125
1	2.05455	1.39983
2	1.87188	.199559
3	1.83568	7.31325E-03
4	1.83425	1.09673E-05

SOLUTION
X = 1.83425
F(X) = 1.09673E-05

OPTION ?35
STOPPING CRITERION ?3
BOTH RESIDUAL AND STEP SIZE

Try a different
stopping criterion

OPTION ?1

NEWTON-RAPHSON METHOD

N	X	F(X)
0	2.5	6.125
1	2.05455	1.39983
2	1.87188	.199559
3	1.83568	7.31325E-03
4	1.83425	1.09673E-05
5	1.83424	4.76837E-07

SOLUTION
X = 1.83424
F(X) = 4.76837E-07

OPTION ?9

DONE

18

4.5 PROBLEMS

Your tutor has notes on each of these problems.

Non-linear Equations

The following problems are on non-linear equations.

1. What are the roots of

$$\tan x = x^2$$

in the interval $[0, 20]$?

2. The roots of the equation

$$\sin x + \frac{x - a}{x + 1} = 0$$

clearly depend on the value of a. Investigate how the smallest root of this equation varies with values of a between 3 and 6.

3. In *Unit 2*, section 2.6.2 and Television Programme 1, we look at the equation

$$\frac{\{\frac{\pi}{8} \sin 5x - \exp[\frac{\pi}{8}(x + 1)^{\frac{1}{2}}] + (x + \frac{5\pi}{8})^{\frac{1}{2}}\} \{1 + \frac{\pi}{8}(x - 1)^2\}^{\frac{1}{2}}}{\{\exp(-x^2) - \frac{\pi}{4}\} \{1 + \frac{\pi}{8}(x + 1)^2\}} + \frac{\pi}{8} = 0$$

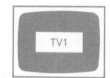

Find all roots of this equation. Since the BASIC expression for this equation exceeds 72 characters, we have already provided it for you with the program $NCROOT. After option 10, when the program types

    F(X) = ?

reply

    PROB3

4. What are roots of the following equation?

$$\log \{\log(\sin x)\} = 0.$$

5. How does the largest root of

$$\sin x - ax = 0$$

vary with a? Tabulate the root for a taking the values 0, 0.25, 0.5, 0.75, 1, 2. Suppose that the value of a is subject to an error ± 0.05. What can you say about the largest root?

6. What are the roots of the following quartic equation?

$$x^4 - 10x^3 + 35x^2 - 50x + 23 = 0.$$

7. How sensitive are the roots of

$$x^4 - 2.40x^3 + 1.03x^2 + 0.60x - 0.32 = 0$$

to changes in the value of the constant term?

8. What is the minimum value of

$$y = \frac{\tan x}{x^2}$$

for x in the interval $[0, \frac{\pi}{2}]$?

9. For values of $a < 1/e$ discuss the number and multiplicity of the roots of

$$xe^{-x} = a$$

Calculate the smallest root for $a = 0.06$.

Linear Equations

The following problems are on simultaneous linear equations.

10. What is the solution of the following system of equations? Are they well-conditioned?

$$
\begin{bmatrix}
4 & -3 & 2 \\
1 & 0 & 6 \\
4 & -1 & -2
\end{bmatrix}
\begin{bmatrix}
x_1 \\
x_2 \\
x_3
\end{bmatrix}
=
\begin{bmatrix}
1 \\
-1 \\
0
\end{bmatrix}
$$

11. Discuss the following system of equations and solve them if possible. These are typical of the equations that arise in partial differential equations.

$$
\begin{bmatrix}
-6 & 2 & 0 & 0 & 0 & 1 & 0 & 0 & 0 & 0 \\
1 & -5 & 1 & 0 & 0 & 0 & 1 & 0 & 0 & 0 \\
0 & 1 & -5 & 1 & 0 & 0 & 0 & 1 & 0 & 0 \\
0 & 0 & 1 & -5 & 1 & 0 & 0 & 0 & 1 & 0 \\
0 & 0 & 0 & 2 & -6 & 0 & 0 & 0 & 0 & 1 \\
1 & 0 & 0 & 0 & 0 & -6 & 2 & 0 & 0 & 0 \\
0 & 1 & 0 & 0 & 0 & 1 & -5 & 1 & 0 & 0 \\
0 & 0 & 1 & 0 & 0 & 0 & 1 & -5 & 1 & 0 \\
0 & 0 & 0 & 1 & 0 & 0 & 0 & 1 & -5 & 1 \\
0 & 0 & 0 & 0 & 1 & 0 & 0 & 0 & 2 & -6
\end{bmatrix}
\begin{bmatrix}
x_1 \\
x_2 \\
x_3 \\
x_4 \\
x_5 \\
x_6 \\
x_7 \\
x_8 \\
x_9 \\
x_{10}
\end{bmatrix}
=
\begin{bmatrix}
1 \\
2 \\
3 \\
3 \\
2 \\
1 \\
0 \\
-1 \\
-1 \\
0
\end{bmatrix}
$$

To use the library program $NCSLE for this problem use option 15. When the program types

```
NAME = ?
```

reply

```
PROB1
```

12. What is the solution to the following problem? Is the solution sensitive to small changes in the coefficients?

$$
\begin{bmatrix}
1 & 1.5 & .75 & .6 & .3 \\
.75 & 1 & .6 & .5 & 1.5 \\
.6 & .75 & .5 & .43 & 1 \\
.5 & .6 & .43 & .37 & .75 \\
.43 & .5 & .37 & .33 & .6
\end{bmatrix}
\begin{bmatrix}
x_1 \\
x_2 \\
x_3 \\
x_4 \\
x_5
\end{bmatrix}
=
\begin{bmatrix}
1 \\
1 \\
1 \\
1 \\
1
\end{bmatrix}
$$

To use the library program $NCSLE for this problem use option 15. When the program types

```
NAME = ?
```

reply

```
PROB2
```

13. The following system of equations is sparse. Should they therefore be solved by an iterative method? If so which method would you use? If not how would you solve them? Would your answer be different if

$$
a_{1,1} = a_{10,10} = 10
$$

or if

$$a_{1,1} = a_{10,10} = 0.0001?$$

$$\begin{bmatrix} 1.99 & 1 & 0 & 0 & 0 & 0 & 0 & 0 & 0 & 0 \\ 1 & 2 & 1 & 0 & 0 & 0 & 0 & 0 & 0 & 0 \\ 0 & 1 & 2 & 1 & 0 & 0 & 0 & 0 & 0 & 0 \\ 0 & 0 & 1 & 2 & 1 & 0 & 0 & 0 & 0 & 0 \\ 0 & 0 & 0 & 1 & 2 & 1 & 0 & 0 & 0 & 0 \\ 0 & 0 & 0 & 0 & 1 & 2 & 1 & 0 & 0 & 0 \\ 0 & 0 & 0 & 0 & 0 & 1 & 2 & 1 & 0 & 0 \\ 0 & 0 & 0 & 0 & 0 & 0 & 1 & 2 & 1 & 0 \\ 0 & 0 & 0 & 0 & 0 & 0 & 0 & 1 & 2 & 1 \\ 0 & 0 & 0 & 0 & 0 & 0 & 0 & 0 & 1 & 1.99 \end{bmatrix} \begin{bmatrix} x_1 \\ x_2 \\ x_3 \\ x_4 \\ x_5 \\ x_6 \\ x_7 \\ x_8 \\ x_9 \\ x_{10} \end{bmatrix} = \begin{bmatrix} 1 \\ 2 \\ 3 \\ 2 \\ 1 \\ 3 \\ 4 \\ 5 \\ 4 \\ 3 \end{bmatrix}$$

To use the library program $NCSLE for this problem use option 15. When the program types

    NAME = ?

reply

    PROB3

14. If you solve a system of equations by an iterative method, you know from *Unit 3*, section 3.7.3 that

$$\mathbf{x} \simeq \mathbf{x}^{(r)} + \frac{\mathbf{\Delta}^{(r)}}{1 - \lambda}$$

and that for sufficiently large r, for each i,

$$\lambda \simeq \frac{\Delta_i^{(r)}}{\Delta_i^{(r-1)}}$$

Using these two results to eliminate λ, we can define a vector $\tilde{\mathbf{x}}^{(r)}$ where each element is given by

$$\tilde{x}_i^{(r)} = x_i^{(r)} - \frac{(x_i^{(r)} - x_i^{(r-1)})^2}{(x_i^{(r)} - 2x_i^{(r-1)} + x_i^{(r-2)})}$$

Under suitable circumstances $\tilde{\mathbf{x}}^{(r)}$ will converge much faster than $\mathbf{x}^{(r)}$. Use this method, which is known as Aitken's method, to find a solution to the set of equations in Problem 13.

15 Solve the set of equations

$$\begin{bmatrix} .45 & .1 & .16 & .09 & .04 & -.54 \\ .47 & .183 & 0 & .18 & -.31 & -.36 \\ .09 & .154 & .653 & .15 & .19 & .36 \\ .5 & .3 & .2 & .3 & -.2 & .2 \\ -.17 & -.177 & -.163 & -.18 & .32 & .08 \\ .29 & .053 & -.762 & .06 & -.41 & 1.26 \end{bmatrix} \begin{bmatrix} x_1 \\ x_2 \\ x_3 \\ x_4 \\ x_5 \\ x_6 \end{bmatrix} = \begin{bmatrix} 1.032 \\ .3656 \\ 1.6286 \\ .74 \\ -.3794 \\ -2.4176 \end{bmatrix}$$

To use the library program $NCSLE for this problem use option 15. When the program types

    NAME = ?

reply

    PROB4

Appendix   Valid BASIC Expressions for Input to Packages

A valid BASIC expression for use with the library program $NCROOT is a combination of the variable X with constants, functions and operators, and the optional parameter A. Spaces are ignored, but the total length must not exceed 72 characters.

Constant

A constant is a positive or negative decimal number whose magnitude is between an approximate minimum of 10^{-38} and an approximate maximum of 10^{38}, or can be zero. Unlike ordinary BASIC expressions, floating point numbers cannot be expressed by using the letter E to denote the exponent.

Functions

Mathematical functions consist of a three letter name followed by an expression in brackets. The following functions are allowed.

ABS	the absolute value of the expression
EXP	the exponential function
INT	the largest integer less than or equal to the value of the expression
LOG	the natural logarithm
SQR	the square root of the expression
SIN	the sine of the expression (in radians)
COS	the cosine of the expression (in radians)
TAN	the tangent of the expression (in radians)
ATN	the arctangent of the expression (in radians)

Here are some examples.

```
TAN(X)
INT(5-X)
ABS(X-A)
```

Operators

The valid operators are as follows.

+	plus
−	minus
*	multiply
/	divide
↑	raise to the power

Expressions involving several operators are evaluated according to the precedence table.

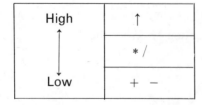

All operators at one level are evaluated before any at the next level. Operators at the same level are evaluated from left to right. Round brackets are used to determine the sequence of evaluating expressions.

Optional Parameter A

In place of a constant the expression may include the optional parameter A. The value of A is set by using option 12 in the program $NCROOT. Here is an example

```
SIN(X)  -  A*X
```

NUMERICAL COMPUTATION COURSE UNITS

1   Introduction to Numerical Methods
2   Non-linear Equations
3   Linear Equations
4   Practical Unit I
5   Linear Programming I
6   Linear Programming II
7   Integer Programming
8   Practical Unit II
9   Approximation I
10 Approximation II
11 Integration
12 Practical Unit III
13 Simulation I
14 Simulation II
15 Practical Unit IV
16 *no text*